M000311531

WHY I'M PROUD TO BE A
REDNECK

101 REASONS

Ellen Patrick

Why I'm Proud to Be a Redneck

Copyright © 2007 Cliff Road Books, Inc.

ISBN-13: 978-1-60261-211-2
ISBN-10: 1-60261-211-0

Jacket and text design by Miles G. Parsons
Printed in Italy

1. Can you say unconditional loyalty?

2. Horse sense
tests at
genius level.

3. Never met a
dog I didn't like.

4. Know when
to hold 'em
and when to
fold 'em.

5. Got my Dollar
Store frequent
buyer card.

6. Know the difference between dinner and supper.

7. Love my truck.

8. Love my family.

9. Love God.

10. Love my country.

11. Never saw
a dirt track I
didn't like.

12. Can you say stock cars?

13. There's more of us than you think.

14. Never saw
a cable TV that
I couldn't
hook up.

15. Hardly ever miss a game.

16. Not everyone appreciates good taxidermy.

17. Not everyone knows how to cook a squirrel.

18. Been driving
since I was
twelve.

19. It ain't a
yard
if you can't
sweep it.

20. The more hair, the better.

21. Fish see me comin' and jump on the hook.

22. Doing my part to fill the world with little rednecks.

23. Got survival honed to a fine art. Just give me a can opener.

24. Hunting
license always
up to date.

25. Know how
to get free
stuff.

26. Know how to name a dog.

27. Know what to do with a remote.

28. Know how to tell a joke.

29. Know how
to call a turkey.

30. Know how to sit on the porch.

31. Know what to do with a snake.

32. Never at a loss for words.

33. Always there for my team.

34. Got more pocket knives than you can count.

35. Got at least two cars up on blocks.

36. Pellet gun champion.

37. Know how to get lost in the woods on purpose.

38. Proud of my license plate collection.

39. Know how to buy in bulk.

40. Got my own
way of fixin'
things.

41. Always having a yard sale.

42. Got my own kind of weather predictin'.

43. Try to be real patient with people that got no sense.

44. Every day is
a good day to
wear boots.

45. Every day is
a good day to
eat corn bread.

46. Every day is a good day for a truck ride.

47. Wrote the book on being true blue.

48. Wrote the book on cleaning my plate.

49. Wrote the book on having seconds.

50. Wrote the book on straight shootin'.

51. Remember all my granddaddy's sayings.

52. Don't much like to leave my home sweet home.

53. Know how
to adjust the
satellite dish in
the dark.

54. Connoisseur of fine quality gasoline.

55. Connoisseur of certain fine beverages.

56. Connoisseur of fine barbecue sauce.

57. Connoisseur of *Wheel of Fortune*.

58. Respect my mamma.

59. Respect my daddy.

60. Am smarter
than
I look.

61. Know the
difference
between right
and wrong.

62. Know the difference between talkin' and saying something.

63. Know the difference between fancy and classy.

64. Know the difference between souped up and fast.

65. Know that, if you can't get there from here, take your ATV.

66. Got a tornado shelter.

67. Got spare parts in the tornado shelter.

68. Got canned tomatoes in the tornado shelter.

69. Got paint cans and antifreeze in the tornado shelter.

70. Got a
garage.

71. Garage is
too full to fit
cars in there.

72. Got more Christmas lights than they got stars in heaven.

73. Keep the Christmas lights up all year 'round.

74. Celebrate every holiday with fireworks.

75. Don't go a day without a Big Gulp.

76. In love with Little Debbie (it's platonic).

77. If you don't like me, you can kiss my grits.

78. Own a fine library of *Sports Illustrated*.

79. Own a fine
collection of
Hank Jr.

80. You can ask
me anything
about NASCAR.

81. Pageants run in our family.

82. Hair spray
runs in our
family.

83. Polyester
runs in our
family – on
Sundays.

84. I know the names of everybody's daddy, mamma, children, and in-laws.

85. Can finish Christmas shopping in one hour at the mall.

86. There's a skinny person in here somewhere.

87. You know you're somebody when you have a County Road address.

88. Grandma lives in an RV out back.

89. Grandma carries a shotgun.

90. Got at least one pet or family member named Dixie.

91. Got at least one pet or family member named Bubba.

92. Got a shed
out back.

93. Got another
shed out back.

94. Pretty much always got somethin' burning in the yard.

95. Expert at chain saw first aid.

96. Carry my lunch in a tool box.

97. Own one of everything they make out of denim.

98. They know me at the landfill.

99. Look good
in camouflage.

100. Nothin' says lovin' like a redneck in the mornin'.

101. There ain't
no better way
to be.